About the Author

Brenda Mills writes from her extensive background in Christian Education. She is a graduate of Moody Bible Institute and received her masters degree in elementary education from Eastern Michigan University. Brenda has worked with children in both public and private schools for twenty years.

In 1974 she became the founding principal and administrator of Grace Community Christian School in Tempe, Arizona. In five years the enrollment grew to 320 elementary students and a staff of 34 teachers.

Brenda is currently the Minister to Children at the First Baptist Church in Pomona, California along with her husband, Larry, who is Minister of Christian Education. They have a son, Nathan, age six.

MY BIBLE STORY PICTURE BOOK

Copyright © 1982 Harvest House Publishers
Eugene, Oregon 97402
Library of Congress Catalog Card Number 82-80509
ISBN 0-89081-319-1

Printed in Hong Kong.

FOREWORD

The greatest heritage we parents can give our children is one that is Bible based, one which will enable them to live a joyful and fulfilled life. The stories embodied in this book will help children to understand who God is and how interested He is in their lives.

You can read these stories from the Scriptures to your child, discuss them and relate them to daily life. It is an excellent teaching tool. Through the parent-child involvement in this book, and through the power of the Holy Spirit you as a parent can instill within a child's heart the desire to believe in Jesus Christ as personal Savior and enjoy the life which God has planned for him.

Read these stories!
Enjoy these stories!
Discuss these stories!

They are a vital part of the Godly heritage which is yours and now made available to your child.

God bless,

Eunice E. Dirks, Director
Early Childhood Education
Association of Christian Schools International

INTRODUCTION

It is exciting to be involved in the world of children! Especially when one has the unique privilege of telling them of God's wonderful love and care!

God's Word contains many beautiful stories that boys and girls are able to comprehend. When comprehension occurs, it is easy to incorporate the truth of the story into one's life. An outstanding theme, or truth, in the Old Testament is obedience. Over and over again God tells His people to obey Him. Likewise, the New Testament's most evident theme is belief in Jesus. Both truths are concepts that are easily understood by children, who, Jesus said, have trusting or believing hearts. (Luke 18:16,17)

My Bible Story Picture Book clearly presents the themes of obedience and belief. As a child is comfortably settled on a loving adult's lap to listen and participate in these stories, it should be natural to discuss these truths as they flow from the stories. Encourage the child's comments! Let them ask questions! As the illustrations bring the characters and stories together, discuss and enjoy them out loud! Do not let the child go away with unanswered questions or unexpressed thoughts. Such sharing and conversation will encourage their own belief in Jesus and their desire to obey God as their Heavenly Father. And we all know that an outcome of respect and obedience to God is respect and obedience to parents and other supervisory adults!

Teachers, too, may use the book in a similar way in a small group setting. The important thing, though, is to involve the listeners in the stories and in the truths they are teaching.

May God use this tool in the hands of loving parents and teachers to further lead little hearts to Jesus.

—Brenda J. Mills

God Makes Our Beautiful World

A long, long time ago there was no world. There was no sky. There was no land. There were no trees or pretty flowers. There was nothing! But God was there. God was always there.

One day God decided to make the world. He made the night and day. He made the sky and the land. He made the beautiful mountains and rivers.

Then God made trees and flowers. He made all the animals. Everything God made was good. The world and everything in it was very beautiful. God was pleased with what He had made. God is a great God!

After God made His beautiful world, He made a man. The man's name was Adam. Adam loved God and obeyed Him. Adam was very happy.

Then God made a woman for Adam. Her name was Eve. She was very pretty. Adam and Eve lived in the beautiful world God made. They had everything they needed to live. They were very happy. They talked to God every day. God was their friend.

(Genesis 1:1-2:25)

Questions:
1) Can God make anything?
2) What made Adam and Eve happy?
3) When you see our beautiful world, you can remember that God made it. Thank God for making our beautiful world.

Adam and Eve Disobey God

All the trees in the garden where Adam and Eve lived gave them all the food they needed. But the tree in the middle of the garden God said they must not eat from. God wanted Adam and Eve to obey Him.

One day Satan, who did not love God, came to the garden. He talked to Eve. He told her a lie about God. He talked her into eating the fruit from the tree God said not to eat from. Eve disobeyed God!

Then Eve gave Adam some of the fruit and he ate it, too. As soon as they ate the fruit, they knew they had disobeyed God. They felt very bad.

How do you feel when you disobey your parents and you know they know you have disobeyed? Yes, you feel very, very bad. This bad feeling is called guilt. Adam and Eve felt guilty.

That evening when God came to visit Adam and Eve in the garden, they hid from Him because they felt guilty. They didn't want God to know they had disobeyed Him. But God always knows. Adam and Eve couldn't hide from God and neither can we. God always knows when we disobey Him. God knows everything.

Because Adam and Eve disobeyed God, He had to punish them. He sent them away from the beautiful garden. Now they had to work hard for their food. Now life was hard. God wants us to always obey Him.

(Genesis 2:15-17; 3:1-19)

Questions:
1) Who caused Eve to disobey God?
2) Why did Adam and Eve feel guilty when God came to talk to them?
3) Did God know Adam and Eve had disobeyed Him?
4) Can you hide your disobedience from God?

Noah Builds an Ark

This man is Noah. The Bible says "Noah walked with God." This means that Noah loved God and obeyed Him. Noah was a good man. He had three sons. Their names were Shem, Ham, and Japheth.

When God looked at the rest of the people in the world, He felt very, very sad. There was no one who loved Him. There was no one who obeyed Him. This saddened God very much. There was no one who loved and pleased God but Noah.

God told Noah to build a big, big boat called an ark. God told Noah and his sons just how to build the boat. They would need this boat because God was going to send a rainstorm and there would be a lot of water all over the world. Noah and his family would be safe on the ark. They would be safe from drowning in the water.

Noah believed God and obeyed Him. He and his sons started to build the ark. It was a lot of hard work, but God was with them. It took a long time. Very soon Noah and his family would be very glad they had obeyed God.

(Genesis 6:9-18)

Questions:
1) What did God tell Noah to do?
2) Why would Noah need an ark?
3) Can a little boy or girl obey God?

God Makes a Promise

When Noah and his sons finished building the ark, God told him to begin gathering together pairs of animals, a mother and a father of each kind. God also told Noah to bring enough food on board the ark to feed his family and all the animals for a long time.

Without asking why, Noah did everything God told him to do. Then one day God told Noah and his family to take all the animals and go aboard the ark. God shut the door behind them! After one week it began to rain. It rained and rained and rained. Soon all the houses, trees, and even the hills and mountains were covered with water. All the people in the world who did not love God drowned. The rain kept coming for forty days and forty nights! But Noah and his family and all the animals were safe on board the ark! They were saved because they believed in God and obeyed Him.

After 150 days, the water began to go away. The ark came to rest on the mountains. After a long time, the ground was finally dry again. God told Noah to go out of the ark. Noah let all the animals go free.

Then Noah prayed and thanked God for keeping them safe. God made Noah a promise that He would never again destroy the world with water. Then God put a beautiful rainbow in the sky to remind all the world of that promise. Now when we see a rainbow, we can think of the promise God made to Noah and all the world and be glad!

(Genesis 6:19-9:17)

Questions:
1) How long did the rains come down?
2) Why were Noah and his family saved?
3) What happened to all the people who did not love God?
4) What promise does the rainbow remind us of?

Abraham Trusts God

Abraham and his wife, Sarah, had been married for many, many years. They did not have any children of their own. They wanted to have a child very badly.

One day God spoke to Abraham. God told him that He would give him a great many blessings. Abraham was then troubled. "If I don't have a son, who will I give all of your blessings to before I die?" he asked God.

God said to Abraham, "You will have a son of your own. He will receive your blessings after you die."

Then God brought Abraham outside and told him to look up at the nighttime sky. There were many, many, many stars in the sky that night. God said to Abraham, "Look up at all those stars. Can you count them?" Abraham knew there were so many stars in the sky that night that they could not be counted.

God said, "Your children's children's children many, many, many years from now will be like that. Too many to count."

Abraham believed what God told him. And because he believed God, God forgave Abraham of all the wrong things he had ever done.

Believing God is called trusting. Abraham trusted God.

(Genesis 15:1-6)

Questions:
1) What did God promise Abraham?
2) How many children's children's children did God say Abraham would have?
3) Did Abraham believe what God said?
4) What does trusting God mean?
5) How can you trust God?

13

God Keeps a Promise to Abraham

One hot summer afternoon Abraham was sitting in the doorway of his tent. He looked down the road. There were three strangers coming! Abraham jumped up and ran to meet the men.

Abraham said hello to them and invited them to come to his camp for some food and rest. The men said they would. Abraham did not know that one of these men was the Lord God!

Abraham ran back to his tent and told his wife Sarah to mix up some pancakes. Then he told his servant to make some delicious meat. Soon he had a good supper of meat, cheese, milk, and bread ready for the men.

As the men ate, one of them said, "Abraham, where is your wife, Sarah?" "Inside the tent," said Abraham.

Then the Lord said to Abraham, "This time next year I will give you and Sarah a little son." Sarah was inside the tent and was listening to the men talk. When she heard the Lord say this, she laughed inside herself. She thought both she and Abraham were too old to have a baby.

The Lord knew it was hard for Sarah to believe they could have a baby. "Is anything too hard for God?" the Lord asked.

It was true. The next year Abraham and Sarah had a baby son. God kept His promise to Abraham. He and Sarah had a baby in their old age!

(Genesis 18:1-14; 21:1-7)

Questions:
1) Who was one of the three visitors?
2) What did the Lord say would happen in one year?
3) What did the Lord say when Sarah didn't believe she could have a baby?

A Wife for Isaac

A braham was now getting very old. His son Isaac was a grown man. One day Abraham called his servant and said, "My son Isaac needs a wife. Please go back to my homeland and find a good girl to be his wife. God will send His angel ahead of you, to make sure you find the right one."

The servant obeyed Abraham. He loaded his camels with food and water for the journey. He also took lovely presents to give to the girl who would become Isaac's wife.

He traveled for many days. Then he arrived at Abraham's homeland. He rested his camels at the village well. It was evening. The women of the village were coming to draw water from the well.

Then the servant prayed, "O God, please show kindness to my master Abraham and help me find a wife for his son Isaac. Please let the girl who offers me, as well as my camels, a drink, be the right girl for Isaac." God heard his prayer.

As soon as he finished praying, a beautiful young girl named Rebekah came to the well. The servant went over to her and said, "Please, may I have a drink?" "Certainly, Sir!" Rebekah said. "And I'll draw water for your camels, too, until they have had enough." He watched her carefully until she had finished. Then he bowed his head and thanked God for answering his prayer.

This beautiful girl, Rebekah, became Isaac's wife. They loved each other and were happy. God blessed them as He had promised Abraham He would do.

(Genesis 24:1-27)

Questions:
1) What did the servant pray the girl would do?
2) Did she do it?
3) How quickly God answered the servant's prayer. Has God ever answered a prayer of yours very quickly?

Jacob and Esau

Isaac and Rebekah had twin sons. Their names were Jacob and Esau. Rebekah loved Jacob the most.

One day when Isaac was very old, he told Esau, the firstborn son, to go hunting, kill a deer, and cook the meat into a delicious stew for him to eat. Then he would give Esau the blessing of the firstborn son.

Rebekah heard Isaac tell Esau this. She wanted Jacob to get the blessing. So she decided to trick Isaac. She made a stew and then had Jacob dress up like Esau. Then Jacob went into Isaac's tent with the stew and pretended to be Esau! Isaac could not see very well, so he believed Jacob and gave him the blessing of the firstborn son!

Then Esau came in with his stew. He did not know that Jacob had tricked his father and had taken his blessing. When Esau found out what Jacob had done, he was very, very angry.

Esau was so angry Rebekah was afraid he would try and kill Jacob. So Rebekah told Jacob to leave home for a while until Esau was no longer angry.

Jacob lied and tricked his father. Such actions are not truthful. God is not pleased when we are not truthful. Because he was not truthful, Jacob had to leave his home and did not see his family for twenty years.

(Genesis 27)

Questions:
1) What blessing did Isaac want to give to Esau?
2) How did Jacob trick Isaac?
3) Why did Rebekah want Jacob to leave home for awhile?
4) Do you think God was pleased with Jacob?

19

The Family of Jacob

Jacob traveled far from his home. He finally arrived at his mother's, Rebekah's, homeland. Jacob stopped to rest beside a well. Some shepherds were resting by the well also. Jacob asked them if they knew a man named Laban, his uncle. "We sure do," they said. "Here comes his daughter Rachel now."

Jacob looked across the field and saw a beautiful young shepherd girl coming to the well to water her sheep. They met, and he told her he was her cousin Jacob. They were both happy to see each other.

Jacob decided to stay and live with his Uncle Laban. Besides, he had fallen in love with the beautiful Rachel. He told Laban, "I'll work seven years for you if you will let Rachel be my wife." It was agreed.

Laban had an older daughter named Leah. The older daughter was supposed to marry first. After Jacob had worked for seven years, he and Rachel were married. But Laban had Leah go into Jacob's tent instead of Rachel. In the dark Jacob did not know it was Leah. When he woke up the next morning and saw it was Leah and not Rachel he was very, very angry with Laban.

But Jacob loved Rachel so much that he worked another seven years for her. Then they were married.

Jacob had twelve sons. These twelve sons became the twelve tribes, or families, through which God kept His promise that his children's children's children many, many years from now would be more than the stars in the sky; too many to count!

(Genesis 37:12-35)

Questions:
1) Who did Jacob go and live with?
2) How long did Jacob work for Rachel?
3) Why did Laban want Leah to be married first?
4) How many sons did Jacob have?

Joseph's Coat of Bright Colors

Jacob had twelve sons. His favorite son was Joseph, because he had been born to Jacob in his old age.

Joseph's job was to help his older brothers watch his father's sheep. He did this every day, and he did a good job.

Because Jacob loved Joseph very much, one day he gave him a special present—a beautiful coat of many bright colors. Joseph was very proud of his coat and wore it every day.

Joseph's brothers were jealous of him because they knew Jacob loved him the most. Then when Jacob gave Joseph the new coat, they were really mad! They really disliked Joseph, and never said any kind words to him.

Because Joseph's brothers were jealous of him, they were very unkind to him. God is not pleased when we are jealous of others. He wants us to be thankful for what we have.

(Genesis 37:2-4)

Questions:
1) Why was Joseph Jacob's favorite son?
2) What special present did Jacob give Joseph?
3) Are jealous feelings good feelings?
4) Is God pleased when we are jealous of others?

Joseph's Brothers' Wicked Plan

One day Joseph's brothers took the sheep far away from home to eat grass. Several days later Jacob told Joseph to go and find them and see how they were getting along.

Joseph finally found his brothers near the town of Dothan. They were still very jealous of him! They did not like him at all! When the brothers saw Joseph coming, they decided to kill him! They said, "Let's kill him and throw him into a deep hole in the ground. Then we'll tell our father, Jacob, that a wild animal has eaten him!" Besides planning to kill Joseph, the brothers were going to tell a lie, too!

But Reuben, the oldest brother, did not want to kill Joseph. He said to the others, "Let's not kill him. Let's throw him into the big hole in the ground; that way he'll die without our killing him!"

When Joseph got to where his brothers were, they pulled off his brightly colored coat and threw him into the big hole in the ground! Then the brothers sat down to eat their supper.

In a little while they saw a camel caravan coming. They were going to faraway Egypt to trade for food. The brothers decided to sell Joseph to the traders on the camel caravan. They sold their brother Joseph for twenty pieces of silver!

Later the brothers killed a little goat and spattered its blood all over Joseph's brightly colored coat. Then they took the coat to their father, Jacob, and told him that a wild animal had killed and eaten Joseph. Jacob believed them! He was very, very sad because he believed Joseph was dead.

(Genesis 37:12-35)

Questions:
1) What did Joseph's brothers want to do to him?
2) What did Reuben talk his brothers into doing instead of killing Joseph?
3) What did they finally do to Joseph?
4) What did the brothers tell Jacob had happened to Joseph?
5) Do you think God was pleased with Joseph's brothers?

God Helps Joseph

When Joseph got to Egypt, he was bought by a rich man named Potiphar, who worked for the king. God was with Joseph and helped him. Joseph did such a good job working for Potiphar that soon he was made the most important worker in Potiphar's house.

One day Potiphar's wife told a lie about Joseph. She said Joseph did something he did not do. So Potiphar had Joseph put in prison.

Joseph was in prison for many years. But even there God was with him and helped him. Once some men in the prison had some strange dreams. They didn't know what the dreams meant. Joseph told them what the dreams meant, and what he said would happen really happened! God helped Joseph to tell what the dreams meant.

Several years later, the king had some dreams. He didn't know what his dreams meant, either. He was very worried. A man who had been in prison with Joseph told the king about Joseph, and how he could tell what dreams meant. The king called for Joseph to be brought to him.

Joseph told the king just what his dreams meant. God helped him to understand the dreams. And what Joseph said would happen really happened! The king was so happy he made Joseph his most important helper in all the land. Joseph loved and obeyed God. And God helped Joseph and kept him safe in this strange new land.

(Genesis 39-41)

Questions:
1) Why did Joseph have to go to prison?
2) How long was he in prison?
3) How did he get out of prison?
4) Who do you think helped Joseph tell what the dreams meant?

Baby Moses

What do you see in this picture? Yes, it is a picture of a little baby in a little basket-boat. Isn't that a strange place for a baby to be? The baby is little Moses. His mother put him in the basket-boat in the tall grass to keep him safe.

The wicked king of Egypt wanted to kill all the boy babies. The king did not love God. Moses' mother and father were some of God's people. The king thought there were getting to be too many of God's people, so he told his soldiers to kill all the boy babies! That way he thought there would not be so many of God's people. So the soldiers wouldn't find baby Moses, his mother hid him the little basket-boat. It floated quietly among the tall grass in the river.

Moses' big sister Miriam hid in the tall grass nearby. She watched the little basket-boat very carefully, and made sure nothing happened to it. She made sure that little Moses was safe.

Soon the king's daughter, the princess, came to the edge of the river with all of her lady helpers. She was going to take a bath there. It was not long before she discovered the little basket-boat floating in the water. She had her helpers bring the little boat over to her. She was very, very surprised when she found out that a little baby boy was inside. She felt sorry for little Moses and decided to take him home with her. Moses lived with the princess until he was a grown man. He was safe from the king. The princess was very good to Moses. She was like a mother to him.

Moses was like a prince, or a king's son, in the land of Egypt. Everybody loved him. He was an important man.

(Exodus 2:1-10)

Questions:
1) Who was the baby in the little basket-boat?
2) Who put him there?
3) How was Miriam helping her mother?
4) Who found little Moses?

29

God Talks to Moses

God's people, who were all of Jacob's sons and their families, had now lived in Egypt for 400 years! There were many, many of them! There was a new king who did not like God's people. He thought there were too many of them. So he made them work very, very hard.

Moses was now a grown-up man. He loved God's people. One day he was out visiting some of his friends. He saw an Egyptian being mean to one of his friends. Moses got mad! He killed the Egyptian and hid his body in the sand!

So Moses had to run away and hide. He knew the king would be angry with him. He went far away from Egypt to live. He lived there for a long time. He married a girl there and had a little baby son.

One day Moses was watching his father-in-law's sheep. He was all alone there with the sheep. He saw a very strange sight up in front of him! A bush was on fire but it wasn't burning up! Moses went closer to see what was happening. (He didn't know that God was going to speak to him from the bush!)

As he got closer, God called, "Moses! Moses!" "Who is it?" Moses asked. "Don't come any closer," God told him, "for you are standing on holy ground."

Then God told Moses that He wanted him to go back to Egypt. There he would become a great leader of God's people. At first Moses was afraid, but finally he told God he would obey. God was with Moses and helped him just as He promised He would. Moses became a great leader for God.

(Exodus 2:11-4:19)

Questions:
1) Why did Moses have to leave Egypt?
2) How did God speak to Moses?
3) What did God tell Moses?
4) Did Moses obey God?

Moses Talks to Pharaoh

In this picture Moses returned to Egypt as God told him to do. Here he is talking to Pharaoh, who is the king.

Moses said to Pharaoh, "God says you must let all His people go free. They must go into the desert, to worship God there."

But Pharaoh did not care what God said. He did not love God. He did not want to let God's people go free because He wanted them to stay in Egypt and work hard for him.

After that Pharaoh made God's people work even harder. Moses went back to Pharaoh many times and asked him to let God's people go free. But he wouldn't.

Then God began to allow terrible things to happen to the Pharaoh and the people of Egypt. The river turned to blood! Bad storms happened! The land was covered with frogs! And then ugly flies! Then all the animals got sick and died! Then big grasshoppers covered all the land! All these awful things happened to the Pharaoh and the Egyptians. But God was with His people. Where they lived, none of these bad things happened. God wanted Pharaoh to let His people go free.

But Pharaoh would not. He wanted God's people to stay in Egypt and work hard for him. He would not listen to Moses, who was speaking for God.

(Exodus 5-10)

Questions:
1) Why didn't Pharaoh want to let God's people go free?
2) What kind of bad things did God let happen?
3) After the bad things happened, did Pharaoh finally let the people of God go free?

God's People Leave Egypt

Pharaoh still would not let God's people leave Egypt. He wanted to make them stay and work hard for him.

God was going to let one more bad thing happen to Pharaoh and the Egyptian people. He was making Pharaoh change his mind to let God's people go free. The oldest boy in every home in Egypt would die that night—even Pharaoh's son! Surely Pharaoh would let God's people go free then!

But God wanted to see if His people would obey Him. So He told Moses to tell the people that each family was to kill a lamb to eat for a special meal. Then they were to take some blood from the lamb and sprinkle the blood all around the doorposts of their house. Then they were to get ready to go on a long journey, ready to leave at any minute.

God's people obeyed what Moses told them to do. That night all the oldest boys in every home of the Egyptians died! There was great sadness everywhere! But all the oldest boys in God's people's homes were safe! When God saw the lamb's blood on the doorposts of their houses, He let the oldest boy live. They lived because God's people obeyed God!

When Pharaoh saw that all the oldest Egyptian boys were dead, he was very sad. So he finally told Moses he could lead God's people out of Egypt!

It was a happy day! There were many, many people walking slowly away from Egypt. They took all their children, their animals, and everything they owned. God took them out of Egypt where they were so unhappy and had to work so hard. They were glad God loved them. They obeyed God.

(Exodus 12:1-51)

Questions:
1) What one last bad thing did God let happen to Pharaoh and the Egyptians?
2) Why didn't God kill the oldest boys in the homes of His people?

35

Food in the Wilderness

Moses and all of God's people traveled in the wilderness for a long time. The people were getting tired. They began to miss all the good food they had in Egypt. They started to complain against God!

This did not please God. But He still loved them very much. He decided to send them special food to eat. They would not even have to work for it!

The next morning all the ground was wet with dew. Dew is what makes the grass wet in the early morning. When the dew disappeared, there were little white flakes all over the ground. When the people saw it, they asked, "What is it?"

The food was called "manna" for that means "what is it?" It was white, like little seeds, and flat, and tasted like honey bread!

Moses said to the people, "This is the food God has given you to eat." Every morning there was always new manna on the ground. All the people had to do was pick it up and save it for their food for that day. So all of God's people had just as much food as they needed every day. No one had too much, and no one had too little. God sent just what they needed for that day.

Not only did God lead His people in the wilderness, but He also gave them food to eat there. All they needed to do was believe God and obey what He told them to do.

(Exodus 16:13-31)

Questions:
1) Why were the people complaining?
2) What was the special food called?
3) What did the food taste like?

God Gives His People Water

After traveling farther into the wilderness, God's people came to a place where there was no water to drink. The people were tired, and wished they had some of the good food and nice things they used to have in Egypt. So they complained again to Moses. Moses got angry with them! "Quiet" he said. "God is really going to get upset with you for complaining."

Because the people were very thirsty, they kept on complaining. "Why did you ever take us out of Egypt?" they asked Moses.

Moses begged God to tell him what to do. God said, "Take the leaders and all the people over to a mountain I will show you. There is a big rock there. I will be there. Hit the rock with your big stick—the same one you held out over the Red Sea."

Moses did as God said. He had learned long ago to always obey God without asking why. When he hit the rock, the good, clear, cool water came pouring out! There was plenty of water for all the people and animals to drink.

Once again the people saw how God took care of them. He gave them water even though they had been complaining and were not thankful. Moses named that place "Meribah," which means "argument." God always gave His people just what they needed, even out in the big, lonely wilderness.

(Exodus 17:1-7)

Questions:
1)   Why did Moses get angry with the people?
2)   Why were the people complaining?
3)   How did God give the people water?

43

The Ten Commandments

Soon God's people arrived at a part of the wilderness called the Sinai Peninsula. There was a big mountain nearby called Mt. Sinai. The people made camp at the bottom of the mountain.

Moses climbed the mountain to meet with God. God called to Moses from somewhere on the mountain and told him He was going to give him some laws for the people to live by. God wrote these laws with His finger on two large stone tablets.

These laws were:
>   You may not love any other God except me.
>   You may not make any gods out of wood or stone.
>   You must not use God's name in the wrong way.
>   Remember the Lord's Day and worship God on that
>   day.
>   Be good and kind to your mother and father.
>   You must not kill.
>   You must not love somebody else's wife.
>   You must not take what is not yours.
>   You must not say what is not true.
>   You must not want what is not yours.

When Moses came down from the mountain, the people said, "You tell us what God says and we will obey."

Then the people saw lightning and smoke coming from the mountain where God had given Moses the laws. They knew God was still there, and they were afraid.

"Don't be afraid," Moses told them, "For God has come in this way to show you His great power, so that from now on you will obey Him!" Then Moses went back up on the mountain to talk to God.

We call the laws God gave to Moses The Ten Commandments. God wants us to obey His laws every day.

(Exodus 19:1-20; 20:1-26)

Questions:
1) Where did Moses go for God to write down the laws?
2) How did God write down the laws?
3) What do we call these laws today?

God's People Disobey

Moses was on the mountain with God for a long time. God gave him a lot of laws to tell to the people. It took forty days and forty nights!

At the bottom of the mountain, the people got tired of waiting for Moses to come down. So some of them went to Aaron, Moses' brother, who was in charge of the people. "Something has happened to Moses," they said. "Make us a god to lead us." They wanted to disobey the very first law God had given them! God said they were not to have any other gods except Him!

So Aaron told the people to bring all their golden earrings to him. He melted the earrings and made a golden calf out of all the gold. The people saw the golden calf and started to worship it like a god. The next day they kept on worshiping the golden calf. They had wild parties and did a lot of things that broke God's laws!

Up on the mountain, God told Moses what the people were doing. God wanted to kill all of them for disobeying Him! But Moses begged Him not to.

Moses went down the mountain. He saw the golden calf and got very angry. He melted the calf and destroyed it. Then he said, "All of you who are on the Lord's side, come over here and join me." These people who joined Moses became leaders in God's service for the rest of their lives.

Later God sent an awful sickness on all the people because they had disobeyed Him by worshiping the golden calf.

(Exodus 32)

Questions:
1) Why did the people want to make a god for themselves?
2) Were they disobeying one of God's laws?
3) What did Moses do to the golden calf?
4) What did God finally do to the people because they worshiped the golden calf?

47

God Tells His People to Obey

Moses told the people all the laws God had given to him. God wanted the people to live by the laws, and to obey them. God promised that if they obeyed all His laws, they would have a good, long life.

God promised also that if they obeyed all His laws they would become a great nation of people. He would give them a rich land "flowing with milk and honey" to live in. God had promised this to Abraham many, many years before. All the people had to do was believe God and obey Him!

Moses told the people they must love God very, very much. They must also remember all God's laws and live by them.

And they were to teach these laws to their children. They were to talk about them every day. When they were at home, or out for a walk, they were to remember them. At bedtime and early in the morning, they were to talk about the laws to their children.

This way God's people's children would grow up believing in and obeying God's laws. He commanded His people to teach His laws to their children. God knows this is very important.

The people were to love God, obey Him, and do what is good and right. If they did, God promised to bless them and make them great.

The same is true for us today. God wants us to believe in Him, to obey Him, and to live to please Him.

(Deuteronomy 6)

Questions:
1) Why did God give the laws to the people?
2) What did God promise to give the people if they would obey Him?
3) How can you obey God?

49

Rahab Helps God's People

Joshua was the leader of God's people now. But before they could go into the Promised Land, they needed to know what kind of people lived there. They needed to know if they were friendly or not.

Joshua sent two men to the city of Jericho. They came into the city and went to a house where people could stay overnight. The woman who owned the house was named Rahab.

The people in Jericho had heard that God's people were camped nearby. They were afraid of them because they had heard stories of the great things God had done for His people. The king of Jericho heard that two men from God's people's camp had come into his city. So he sent the police to check it out.

Rahab was friendly to the two men. She had heard about God's people and thought their God must be very great. So she hid the two men from the police. She hid them on the roof of her house under some plants that were drying there. When the policemen came to her house and asked about the men, she said they were there before, but now had gone away. The policemen believed her and left.

Later that night Rahab went up on the roof to talk to the two men. She told them she believed their God would help them take over the city. The men thanked her and promised that when their people took over the city she and all her family would be saved. Then she let them down off her roof by a long rope.

The two men went back to their camp. They told Joshua all that happened. They said that the people in Jericho were afraid of God's people. It would be an easy city to take over.

(Joshua 2)

Questions:
1) Who was the woman that hid the two men?
2) Why were the people in Jericho afraid of God's people?
3) Did the two men think Jericho would be easy to take over?

Jericho's Walls Fall Down

The gates of the city of Jericho were kept shut. The people of Jericho knew God's people were camped nearby. They were afraid of what God's people would do to them.

But God had already told Joshua's people that He was going to give them the city! God said they wouldn't have to fight a battle to get it!

God told Joshua to have His army march around the city of Jericho once a day for six days. They were to be followed by seven priests, each carrying a horn called a trumpet. On the seventh day, they were to walk around the city seven times, blowing their trumpets all the time. Then when the priests gave one long blast from their trumpets, everyone was to shout out loud! Then God would make the high stone walls all around the city fall down!

And that is just what happened! The people inside the city were very, very scared. They didn't know what God's people were doing. They were confused! Then when the people shouted, the walls all fell crashing down to the ground! God's people ran into the city and killed all the people who did not believe in God. Then they burned that wicked city to the ground!

But Rahab and her family were saved. She was saved because she believed in God and because she hid the two men who came to check out the city. She and her family went to live outside the camp of God's people.

(Joshua 6:1-25)

Questions:
1) What did God tell Joshua to have the army do?
2) God said He would give His people the city without a battle. Did they have to fight?
3) What people in the city were saved?

53

Gideon, a Good Leader for God

Gideon was a young man that God had chosen to be a leader in His people's army. He was a good leader. He trusted God to help him win battles.

Gideon and his army were getting ready for a big battle against the army of some people who did not love God. God said to Gideon, "You have too many men in your army. If you win the battle, they will say they won the fight themselves. They will not believe I helped them win."

God told Gideon to send home all those men who were scared to fight. Many, many men left!

The rest of the army God told Gideon to have go down to a little river. God was going to give them a test to see if they would make good soldiers. Gideon told the men to drink water from the little river. He watched them carefully as they did.

Most of the men got down on their knees and drank with their mouths down in the water. God told Gideon to send all these men home.

But 300 men bent over and cupped up some water in their hands and drank. That way, they were better soldiers. They could run away quickly if strange soldiers surprised them suddenly. God said they would make the best soldiers.

They were the ones God used to win a big battle over some people who didn't love God. Gideon was a good leader and God gave him good soldiers. But God always won the battles for His people.

(Judges 7:1-7)

Questions:
1) Why didn't God want many men in Gideon's army?
2) What test did God give the men drinking water at the river?
3) Do you think Gideon had the best soldiers?
4) Who really helped Gideon win battles?

The Prayer of Hannah

Hannah was a lady who loved God very much. She was a married lady, but she and her husband did not have any children. Hannah wanted to have a little son very much.

At a special holiday time, Hannah went to God's house to pray. She was very sad because she wanted a little baby of her own. So she talked to God about it. She told God in her prayer that if He would give her a little son she would give him back to God and let him be a helper in God's house all his life. Hannah really meant her prayer!

As soon as she finished her prayer, Hannah felt much better. She did not feel so sad any more. She seemed to know that God had heard her prayer. And she believed that God would answer her prayer, too!

So Hannah went back to her family and enjoyed the holiday time. She was not sad any more. And about one year later, God answered her prayers! Hannah had a little son! She named him Samuel. He was a special little boy to her, because she had asked God for him!

(I Samuel 1:1-18)

Questions:
1) Why did Hannah go to pray in God's house?
2) What did she pray for?
3) Why did Hannah feel better right after she prayed?
4) Did God answer her prayer?

God Talks to Samuel

Hannah's little son, Samuel, was soon old enough to be taken to God's house to live. Hannah kept her promise to God.

So Hannah took little Samuel to live with Eli, the preacher in God's house. Samuel missed his mother, but he was happy being a helper in God's house. And every year his mother visited him and brought him a new little coat!

One night Samuel went to bed as usual. He had only been in bed a little while when he heard someone call, "Samuel, Samuel!" He thought Eli was calling him. Samuel obeyed Eli. So he ran to Eli's bed and said, "Did you call me?" Eli said, "No, Samuel, I did not call you." So Samuel went back to his own bed.

In a little while, Samuel heard the voice again, "Samuel, Samuel!" Again Samuel went to Eli. Again Eli told him that he did not call.

For the third time, the voice called Samuel. He ran to Eli and said, "Yes, what do you need?" This time Eli knew it was the Lord who was calling Samuel. Eli said, "Go and lie down. If the voice calls again say, 'Yes, Lord, I'm listening.'" So Samuel went back to bed.

Sure enough, the Lord called Samuel again, "Samuel, Samuel!" This time Samuel said, "Yes, Lord, I'm listening to you."

The Lord told Samuel that He was going to punish all the people who did not love Him and obey Him. Samuel listened to God, obeyed Him, and became one of God's greatest workers.

(I Samuel 2:11-19; 3:1-14)

Questions:
1) Who did Samuel think was calling him?
2) What did God finally tell Samuel?
3) Samuel listened to God. God speaks to us today when we read the Bible. We should make sure we listen to God like little Samuel did.

59

David and Goliath

The Philistines were God's people's enemies. The two peoples were at war with each other. King Saul was now the leader of God's people's army. His army was camped on one hill, and across a big valley the army of the Philistines was camped on another hill.

The Philistines had a very big soldier named Goliath. He was a giant! He wore lots of heavy armor to protect himself from arrows when he was fighting. Every day he went down to the valley and yelled for King Saul to send someone down to fight him. Not many people wanted to fight Goliath!

One day David, a little shepherd boy, came to the army camp to bring his brothers some food. He heard the giant bragging about how strong he was. He was making fun of the men in King Saul's army. David wanted to fight Goliath. At first King Saul didn't want him to, but finally said he could. "And may the Lord be with you," the king said to him.

David went to a little stream and found five smooth stones. He put them in his shepherd's bag. He had only his shepherd's staff and his sling to fight the giant with! When Goliath saw David, he made fun of him. David said, "You come with a sword and a spear, but I come in the name of the Lord."

David put a little stone in his sling, slung it around his head, and the stone went flying through the air. It hit Goliath right in the middle of his forehead, and he fell to the ground dead!

The mighty Philistine army turned and started to run away. They were afraid now that their giant was dead.

(I Samuel 17)

Questions:
1) What was the name of the giant?
2) Why do you think King Saul's soldiers were afraid to fight him?
3) How did David kill Goliath?
4) Who do you think helped David?

Solomon and the Two Mothers

Solomon was King David's son. When he became king after his father died, he asked God for a special gift.

King Solomon asked God for an understanding heart. He wanted to be a wise, good ruler of God's people. He asked God to show him what was right and what was wrong.

God was pleased with King Solomon's prayer. God gave him what he asked for. God also made him the richest king God's people had ever had! He was a good, wise, kind king.

One day two mothers came to King Solomon. They were having an argument. They wanted King Solomon to settle the argument for them.

One mother said, "We live together in our house. Not long ago I had a baby. A few days later, this other woman had a baby, too. But she rolled over on her baby in bed one night and it died. When she saw it was dead, she put the dead baby by me and took my live baby. When morning came, I saw what she had done. I want my baby back!"

The other woman said, "She's not telling the truth! The baby is mine!" So they kept on arguing.

King Solomon said, "Bring me a sword. We'll cut the live baby in half and give one half to one mother and the other half to the other mother."

Then the woman who really was the mother of the baby said, "Oh, no, Sir, give her the baby. Don't kill him!" The other woman said, "All right, it will be neither yours nor mine! Divide it between us!"

King Solomon said, "Give the baby to the woman who wants it to live. She is the mother of the child."

The wise king knew that the real mother would give the baby to another woman before she would let it be killed. He knew she really loved the baby.

King Solomon always used his great wisdom to do what was right and what pleased God.

(I Kings 3:6-28)

Questions:
1) What was King Solomon's special prayer to God?
2) What else did God give him besides wisdom?
3) What were the two women arguing about?
4) How did King Solomon settle their argument?

Elijah and the Poor Widow

Elijah was a prophet. A prophet is someone who tells what God is going to do. Elijah loved God and served Him well.

Once God told Elijah to go to a certain town. There he saw a poor woman whose husband was dead. She lived alone with her only son. The woman was gathering sticks to build a fire. She was very poor.

When Elijah saw her, he asked her for a cup of water to drink. As she was going to get it, he asked her to bring him some bread, too. "But Sir," she said, "I don't have any bread left in my house. I just have a little handful of flour and a little cooking oil. I was gathering a few sticks to build a fire. I was going to bake some bread for our last meal. Then my son and I will die. We have no other food!"

Elijah said to her, "Don't be afraid! Go ahead and cook your last meal. But bake me a little loaf of bread first. There will still be enough for you and your son. The Lord God says if you do this there will always be plenty of oil and flour for you to bake bread with until He gives you other food."

And what Elijah said really happened! The woman and her son kept on using the flour and oil to bake bread. No matter how much they used, there always was plenty left in the jars, just like God had told Elijah!

(I Kings 17:8-16)

Questions:
1) What is a prophet?
2) How do you know the woman was very, very poor?
3) What did Elijah tell her to do?
4) Did the woman believe Elijah?

Elisha and the Pots of Oil

One day a woman whose husband had died came to Elisha, the prophet. Her husband loved God, but he had owed someone some money when he died. Now that person said if the woman did not pay the money her husband owed, he would have her and her two sons put in jail! "What shall I do?" she asked Elisha.

"How much food do you have in the house?" Elisha asked her. "Not much. Just a jar of olive oil," she said.

Then Elisha told her to do a strange thing. He said to go to all her friends and borrow as many empty pots and pans as she could find. Then she and her sons were to take all the pots and pans, go inside their house, and shut the door. Then they were to pour olive oil from their jar into all the pots and pans.

They did as they were told. The sons kept bringing pots and pans and the woman kept filling them up. There seemed to be no end to the olive oil in her jar! All the pots and pans she had were filled to the brim!

"Bring me some more jars," she told her sons. "We can't find any more," they said. And when they stopped bringing more jars and pots and pans, the oil stopped flowing!

Then Elisha told her to take the oil and sell it and use the money to pay back the money her husband owed. She did so and she and her sons did not have to go to jail! There was also enough money left over for them to live on! They believed what God's servant Elisha said to do and God gave them what they needed!

(II Kings 4:1-7)

Questions:
1) What had happened to the woman?
2) What did Elisha tell her to do?
3) When did the oil stop flowing from the woman's jar?

Naaman Believes God

Naaman was the leader of the army of the land of Syria. Syria was a country that did not worship the Lord God. The army of Syria would often take God's people prisoners. They made the captured people work for them. In Naaman's house there lived such a little girl. She worked for Naaman's wife as her maid, or a helper, in the house.

Naaman was also a leper. A leper is someone who has the awful disease of leprosy. The doctors did not know how to make a person who had leprosy get well. Lepers got very sick and then finally died.

The little girl who worked for Naaman's wife loved God. She also knew that often God used His prophet Elisha to help people. So she told Naaman's wife about Elisha. Naaman wanted to be made well!

So he went to see Elisha. Elisha sent a messenger out and told Naaman to go down and wash seven times in the Jordan River and he would be made well of all his leprosy. That made Naaman really angry! He thought that was too easy. But the men in his army talked him into doing just what Elisha said to do.

Naaman went down to the Jordan River. One, two, three, four, five, six times he dipped his body down under the water. And after the seventh time, his whole body was made clean and well! The leprosy was completely gone!

He went back to Elisha and said, "Now I know at last that there is no God in all the world except your God." And he believed in God!

(II Kings 5:1-17)

Questions:
1) What disease did Naaman have?
2) Who told Naaman about Elisha?
3) What did Elisha tell Naaman to do?
4) Why do you think Naaman believed in God?

Job Believes and Loves God

Job was a good man who loved God. God blessed him with a large family and a lot of riches. He owned many large herds of animals. He was the richest man around!

Once God allowed all of Job's family to be killed. He also allowed Job to lose all of his animals and riches. Then God allowed Job to be covered all over his body with big, awful sores!

Job was very, very sad. The sores on his body hurt a lot. But through all this he still loved God. He said, "Everything I had was given to me by God. If He wants to take it all away, it's all right with me." Job did not get angry with God nor disobey Him.

Job's friends told him that surely he must have disobeyed God for all these bad things to happen to him. Job's wife even told him to tell God he didn't love Him anymore!

But Job still loved God. He believed God was great and mighty. He kept on believing in God through all the hard times.

And God was pleased with Job! Now God knew that Job really loved Him, no matter what He let happen to him. So God blessed Job again. He was made well. The awful sores left his body. And the Lord gave him another large family and twice as many animals as he had before! Job was once more very, very rich. It was God that gave Job everything he had. Job knew that. God let him live a long, good life.

(Job 1 and 42)

Questions:
1) Where did all of Job's riches come from?
2) What did God let happen to Job?
3) Did Job get upset with God?
4) What did God give Job again?

Jonah and the Great Fish

God told Jonah to take a message to the city of Nineveh. God was going to destroy the city and all the people there because they were so wicked!

But Jonah was afraid. He did not want to go to Nineveh. So he disobeyed God! He ran away! He went down to the sea, to the city of Joppa. There he bought a ticket and got on board a ship headed for another city. He went to the very bottom of the ship, hoping to hide from God!

The Lord knew just where Jonah was. We can never hide from God, and neither could Jonah! So God caused a big storm to come. The ship was tossed about on the sea. The sailors thought they would all drown!

Jonah finally told them that he was running away from God. The men were very scared of the storm. So Jonah told them to throw him into the sea and then the storm would stop.

But Jonah did not drown! God prepared a great fish to swallow him. He was inside the fish for three days and three nights! While he was there he had time to think and pray. He told God he was sorry for running away. He thanked God for saving him from drowning. And the Lord ordered the fish to spit Jonah up onto the beach!

Jonah then obeyed God and went to the wicked city of Nineveh. He told the people about God and how He was going to destroy the city. The people told God they were sorry for all their sins.

(Jonah 1-3)

Questions:
1) Why did God want Jonah to go to Nineveh?
2) What did Jonah do instead?
3) What did God do to Jonah to get him to obey Him?
4) What lesson can you learn from Jonah?

Daniel in the Den of Lions

Daniel was a favorite helper of the king. Other men became very jealous of him because the king liked him so well.

The men who were jealous of Daniel talked the king into making a special order. It said that anyone who prayed to any god except the king would be thrown into a den of lions! The king signed his name to the order and it became a law. That meant it could not be changed!

The wicked men knew that Daniel prayed three times a day to God. After the order was passed, he still prayed to God. He would never pray to a man! The men who were jealous of Daniel caught him praying and told the king.

Even though the king loved Daniel, he had to keep his word. He had Daniel thrown into the den of lions!

The king couldn't sleep all night. Early the next morning he went over to the den of lions. He called "O Daniel, servant of the living God! Was your God able to save you from the lions?"

Then the king heard a voice! It was Daniel! "My God has sent His angel to shut the lions' mouths so they can't hurt me." The king was very happy!

Then the king had the men who were so jealous of Daniel thrown into the lions' den. Then he wrote a letter to all the people in the land telling them what a great God Daniel's God was!

(Daniel 6)

Questions:
1) Why were the other men jealous of Daniel?
2) What was the king's special order?
3) Why do you think Daniel didn't obey the king's order?

Jesus Is Born

Mary and Joseph had been traveling for many days. They were very tired and so was the little donkey on which Mary was riding. They were glad when they reached the little town of Bethlehem.

The town was very crowded with people. Joseph looked all over for a place where he and Mary could spend the night. It was very important that they find a place soon, for Mary was going to have a baby!

Everywhere they looked, they got the same answer: "We don't have any room." Finally Joseph found an innkeeper who said he and Mary could sleep out back of his house in a little shelter where he kept his animals. They thanked him and went there. They were very glad for a place to rest.

That night Mary's little baby was born. That baby was Jesus, God's only Son! He was born in a stable where donkeys, cows, and chickens slept! Mary wrapped little Jesus in a blanket and laid him in a manger, the place where cows eat their hay.

That was a wonderful night! God sent His only Son, Jesus, into the world! He came as a little baby. God loved us very, very much! That wonderful night was the very first Christmas!

(Luke 2:1-7)

Questions:
1) Why did Mary and Joseph have to stay in a stable?
2) What was Jesus' bed?
3) Babies are born every night. What was so special about Jesus' birth?

Shepherds Find Baby Jesus

One night some shepherds were taking care of their sheep on a hillside. Nearby was the little village of Bethlehem. It was very, very quiet and still. It was hard for the shepherds to stay awake! Suddenly, a bright light shone out of the sky! The shepherds were very, very scared! They didn't know what was happening. All of a sudden an angel was there with them! "Don't be afraid," he said, "I have good news for you. Jesus has been born tonight in Bethlehem. You will find him wrapped in a blanket, lying in a manger."

Then many, many other angels could be seen in the sky. They all sang, "Glory to God in the highest heaven, and peace on earth for all those pleasing Him." Then it was quiet again.

The shepherds said to each other, "Come, let's go and find baby Jesus!" They ran quickly to Bethlehem and found the baby Jesus, lying in a manger, just like the angel had said. The shepherds were very glad! Then they ran and told everyone in the village that Jesus had been born.

(Luke 2:8-16)

Questions:
1) Who told the shepherds Jesus had been born?
2) Did the shepherds obey the angel?
3) Why do you think the shepherds ran and told everyone that Jesus had been born?

Jesus Goes to God's House

This is Jesus when He was a young boy. He lived with His parents, Mary and Joseph. They lived in the little village of Nazareth. Joseph was a carpenter. A carpenter is someone who makes things out of wood. Jesus helped Joseph in his carpenter's shop. Jesus was a good helper. Jesus always obeyed Mary and Joseph.

Jesus worked hard. He grew tall. He was also very wise. All the people who knew Jesus loved Him. God in heaven also loved Jesus. God was very pleased because Jesus was a good boy.

Jesus liked to go to God's house. He liked to talk with the preachers and teachers there. They were always surprised at how much Jesus knew about God. They did not know Jesus was God's own Son!

One time Mary and Joseph thought Jesus was lost. They looked everywhere for Him! Finally, they found Him in God's house, talking with the preachers and teachers about God. Mary and Joseph were very happy when they found Jesus.

(Luke 2:41-52)

Questions:
1) Where did Jesus' family live when He was a young boy?
2) How did Jesus help Joseph?
3) When Jesus was lost, where did Mary and Joseph find Him?
4) Do you like to go to God's house?

Jesus Calls His Disciples

Now Jesus spent all His time teaching and preaching to people. He was very busy. He knew He had to have some special friends to help Him in His work of telling people about God.

One day Jesus chose twelve men to be His special friends. They were followers of Jesus. They believed He was God's Son. They believed in everything He did. They were called disciples.

The name of Jesus' disciples were:

Simon Peter	Bartholomew
James	Matthew
John	Thomas
Andrew	James, the son of Alphaeus
Philip	Thaddeus
Simon	Judas Iscariot

These men left their homes and families and traveled with Jesus. Jesus taught them many things. He taught them about God. He taught them about people. He taught them to work as His helpers.

The disciples loved Jesus very much. They loved Him more than their homes and families. They loved Jesus best of all.

(Mark 3:13-19)

Questions:
1) What is a disciple?
2) Can you say the names of Jesus' disciples?
3) How much did the disciples love Jesus?
4) Do you love Jesus best of all?

Peter Believes in Jesus

One day Jesus was preaching on the shores of a big lake. There were many, many people there listening to Him. The group of people got bigger and bigger and began to crowd Jesus.

At the edge of the water stood two empty fishing boats. Some fishermen were nearby washing their fishing nets. Jesus stepped into one of the boats. Then He asked the boat's owner, Simon Peter, if he would push the boat out into the water a little ways. Peter did what Jesus asked. Then Jesus preached to the people from the little boat. That way it wasn't so crowded.

When Jesus finished preaching, he said to Peter, "Take the boat out into the deep water. Then let down your nets and you will catch a lot of fish." Peter said to Jesus, "But we fished all night and didn't catch a single fish. But if you say to, we will!"

The little boat sailed out to the deep water. The fishermen put their nets down into the water. When they brought them up this time, the nets were so full of fish they began to tear! The little boat was so full of fish that it almost sank! Peter yelled for some other fishermen, James and John, to come and help them bring in all those fish!

When Peter saw all that was happening, he was amazed! He fell on his knees before Jesus!

Jesus said, "Don't be afraid, Peter. From now on you'll be fishing for the souls of men. You'll be telling them about God and how they can love Him."

(Luke 5:1-10)

Questions:
1) Why did Jesus get into the little boat?
2) What did Jesus tell Peter to do?
3) Why was Peter so amazed?
4) Do you think Peter believed in Jesus?

Jesus Makes a Lame Man Well

One day Jesus was teaching some people in a house in a little village. There was a big crowd of people inside the house and outside on the street. They were all listening to Jesus.

Down the road came some men. On a sleeping mat, they were carrying a man who could not walk. A person who cannot walk is called a lame person. The men tried to push their way through the crowd to get to Jesus, but they couldn't get through.

The men carrying the lame man were very smart! They went up on the roof of the house. Then they took off some tiles from the roof to make a big hole. They carefully lowered the lame man down to Jesus! He was still lying on his sleeping mat!

It was very important for these men to get their lame friend to Jesus. They believed Jesus could make him walk again. They believed Jesus could make him completely well.

When Jesus saw how much they believed, he said to the lame man, "My friend, your sins are forgiven."

Some men in the crowd who didn't believe in Jesus said, "Who can forgive sins but God?" They didn't know Jesus was God's Son. Then, to prove He was God's Son, Jesus made the lame man walk again! He said, "Pick up your sleeping mat and go on home; you are now well!"

While everybody watched, the man jumped up, picked up his sleeping mat, and ran home, praising God all the way! Jesus did wonderful things like this to show people He really was God's Son.

(Luke 5:18-26)

Questions:
1) What was wrong with the man on the sleeping mat?
2) How did his friends get him to Jesus?
3) Why did Jesus do wonderful things like making the lame man well again?
4) Do you believe Jesus is God's Son?

87

The Wind and Water Obey Jesus

Jesus had been teaching people all day. He was tired. He wanted to get away from all the people and rest. He and His disciples got into a little boat and started to cross the lake. They wanted to cross to the other side to get away from the crowds of people.

When they were in the middle of the lake, suddenly a terrible storm came up! The wind blew! The lightning crashed! The thunder roared! The waves got higher and higher! The disciples were scared! They thought surely the little boat would sink and they would all drown!

All the while, Jesus was sleeping peacefully in a corner of the boat. The disciples went to Him and woke Him up. They shouted, "Lord, save us! We're sinking!"

But Jesus was disappointed that they were so afraid. They should have believed He would take care of them.

Then He stood up and held out His arms. "Peace! Be still!" he ordered the wind and the water. Suddenly, the lake was quiet and still once more.

The disciples just sat in the boat, hardly able to believe what they had just seen. "What kind of man is this," they asked each other, "that even the wind and water obey Him?"

Jesus could do wonderful things because He is God's Son. He did all these things so that people would believe He was God's Son.

(Matthew 8:18-27)

Questions:
1) Why did Jesus want to get away from the people?
2) What was Jesus doing while it was storming?
3) What did Jesus say to the storm?
4) Why did Jesus do wonderful things like stopping the storm?

The Story of the Good Samaritan

O nce Jesus told a story about a man who went on a journey. He was traveling along on his little donkey, on a lonely part of the road. Suddenly some robbers jumped out from behind some rocks where they had been hiding. They hit the man hard on his head and body till he fell to the ground badly hurt. Then they took all his money and his good clothes. They even stole his little donkey and all his food! Then they just left him lying there hurt on the ground.

Soon a priest from God's house came by. He pretended he didn't see the man there on the ground. He just walked on by! Then another man who worked as a helper in God's house came along. He, too, walked on by and didn't even stop to help the hurting man. These men were afraid that the robbers might still be nearby and if they stopped to help the man on the ground, the robbers might hurt them, too. They thought only of themselves!

Soon a man from the country of Samaria came by. He was supposed to be an enemy of the hurt man. But as soon as he saw the man lying there, he stopped and helped him! He washed his face, put medicine on his cuts, and gave him some fresh water to drink. Then he helped him onto his own little donkey and took him to a place where he could sleep for the night. He even paid his bill!

This man from Samaria was a very kind man. We call him the Good Samaritan. Jesus wants us to be kind to each other. He wants us to be kind to those people who don't like us, too!

(Luke 10:30-37)

Questions:
1) How did the kind man help the hurt man?
2) How can you be kind to someone today?

The Boy Who Gave His Lunch
to Jesus

One day Jesus spent the day on a lovely hillside teaching people about God. There were many, many people there. There were moms and dads, little children, big kids, and grandmas and grandpas. There were many, many more people than you could ever count! They had listened to Jesus most all day, and now it was suppertime. The people were getting hungry.

Jesus' helpers told Him to tell the people to go home, so they could get some supper. Jesus said, "They do not need to leave; you give them some food." One little boy had remembered to bring his lunch with him. He had not eaten it yet. He had five little loaves of bread and two small fish. The boy gladly gave his lunch to Jesus.

Jesus told the people to get ready to eat. Then He took the boy's lunch and thanked God for it. Then He shared the food and gave it to His helpers. They passed it out to the people. There was enough food for all those hungry people to eat! And there was even some left over! Jesus made the food grow so there would be enough for all. Jesus was able to do this because He is God's Son!

(Matthew 14:14-21)

Questions:
1) Who gave his lunch to Jesus?
2) What was the lunch?
3) Was there enough food for all the people?
4) Who is Jesus?
5) Do you remember to thank God for all the good food you have to eat?

Peter Walks on the Water

I t was evening time. Jesus had been teaching the people all day. He needed to go away and talk to God in prayer. He told His disciples to get in their little boat and cross to the other side of the lake. He would meet them there later. Then Jesus went up into the hills to pray by Himself.

Darkness came. A storm blew up on the lake. The wind blew hard! The waves got bigger and bigger!

Suddenly the disciples saw a strange figure coming toward them, walking on the water. They screamed, for they thought it was a ghost! But it was Jesus! He was walking on the water, coming to them! "Don't be afraid," he said, trying to keep them from being frightened.

Peter said to Jesus, "Sir, if it really is you, tell me to come over to you, walking on the water!" "All right," Jesus said to him, "come along!"

So Peter slid carefully over the side of the boat, and walked on the water toward Jesus! He was doing fine, looking at Jesus and walking toward Him on the water. Then he remembered the high waves and the deep water. He took his eyes off Jesus and looked at the water all around him. He suddenly got very scared and started to sink! "Jesus! Save me!" Peter shouted.

Jesus reached out His hand and saved Peter from drowning. Then He said, "Peter, why didn't you believe me?" Then they climbed back into the little boat and the storm stopped.

The other disciples who had been watching all this could hardly believe what they had seen. They said to Jesus, "You really are the Son of God!"

(Matthew 14:21-33)

Questions:
1) At first, did the disciples know who was walking on the water toward them?
2) When did Peter begin to sink?
3) Why do you think Jesus did wonderful things like walking on the water?

Jesus Makes Lazarus Alive Again

Lazarus lived in the village of Bethany with his sisters Mary and Martha. They were all good friends of Jesus. They loved Jesus very much. He stayed in their home in Bethany many times.

One time Jesus was in another town and word came to him that Lazarus was very sick. Jesus waited on purpose for two days before going to Bethany to see Lazarus. He wanted to have another chance to show the people that He really was the Son of God. When he finally arrived just outside the village, Martha ran to meet Him and said, "Sir, if you would have been here, my brother would not have died." Jesus was very sad to hear that Lazarus had died. "Your brother will come back to life again," he said to Martha.

There were a lot of church leaders at Mary and Martha's home. Then when Mary came out to meet Jesus too, they followed her. Mary, too, said to Jesus, "Sir, if you would have been here, my brother would still be alive!"

Jesus said, "Where is he buried?" The church leaders said, "Come and see." Tears came to Jesus' eyes. He loved Lazarus very much.

They came to the place where Lazarus was buried. It was a little cave. Jesus said, "Roll the stone door aside!" So they rolled the stone aside. Then Jesus prayed and thanked God for hearing His prayer. Then He shouted, "Lazarus, come out!" Jesus made Lazarus alive again! He was still wrapped in graveclothes! Jesus said, "Unwrap him and let him go!"

Many people believed Jesus was God's Son when they saw this wonderful thing that Jesus did.

(John 11:1-45)

Questions:
1) Why do you think Jesus waited two days before going to see Lazarus?
2) Do you think Mary and Martha thought Jesus could make Lazarus alive again?
3) Why did Jesus do wonderful things like this?

Jesus Loves the Little Children

Once some mothers brought their babies and little children to Jesus. They wanted Him to bless them.

Jesus was very busy. There were a lot of people around Him. His disciples scolded the mothers for bringing the children to Jesus. They thought Jesus was much too busy to be bothered with little children. They told the mothers to take their children back home.

But Jesus heard them. He said to His disciples, "Let the little children come to me. Never send them away! For the kingdom of God belongs to men who have hearts as believing as these little children. And anyone who doesn't have their kind of belief will never get to heaven."

Jesus loved the little children. He took time to talk to them. Some of them sat on His lap. He held the tiny babies in His arms. He was never too busy for children!

Aren't you glad that Jesus loves children? Aren't you glad that a little child can believe in Jesus?

(Luke 18:15-17)

Questions:
1) Why did the disciples try and send the children away?
2) What did Jesus tell His disciples about children?
3) Did Jesus send children away?
4) As a little child, you can believe in Jesus. You can believe Jesus is God's only Son. Do you believe in Jesus?

The Leper Who Said "Thank You" to Jesus

T he men running away in this picture had a bad sickness called leprosy. The doctors did not know how to make people sick with leprosy get well. Other people ran away when the lepers came near. They were afraid they would get sick with leprosy, too.

One day Jesus came to their town. The lepers had heard that Jesus loved people and made sick people well. When they saw Jesus they ran to him and begged Him to make them well.

Jesus felt sorry for the sick lepers. Then He told them to go to the temple and tell the ministers there that they were well. The temple was the place where the people worshiped and prayed to God.

The lepers did as Jesus told them. But one looked down at his hands while he was running away. He saw that they were well now. He turned around and went back to Jesus. He told Jesus "Thank You" for making him well. The other men forgot to say "Thank You" to Jesus.

(Luke 17:11-19)

Questions:
1) What is a leper?
2) Who made the lepers in this story well?
3) Did they all thank Jesus?
4) What things can you thank Jesus for?

The Poor Woman's Gift

One time a very poor woman came to God's house. She brought her offering with her to give to God. An offering is your gift to God.

Jesus was there in God's house. He was watching the people give their offerings to God. Jesus watched as the poor woman gave her offering. She placed two small coins into the offering box.

Some rich men came by. They, too, had brought their offerings to God. They brought big, fat bags of money! They gave this money as an offering to God.

After Jesus watched this, he said that the poor woman had given much more than the rich man. After she had given her offering, she didn't have any money left. She had given everything she had! But after the rich men gave their offering, they still had lots of money left over. That was why the poor woman's gift was the biggest and the best.

The poor woman gave everything she had to give. She loved God very, very much to give everything. Jesus told His friends that this is the kind of giving that pleases God the most.

(Mark 12:41-44)

Questions:
1) How much money did the poor woman give?
2) Who did Jesus say gave the most money?
3) Do you give some money to God as a gift each time you go to His house?

The Lord's Supper

The time for the special holiday called Passover had come. This was the time God's people ate a special meal that helped them remember how good God had been to them.

Jesus wanted to eat the Passover meal with His disciples. He knew the time for Him to die would be soon. He wanted to spend this time with His special friends.

Jesus sent Peter and John to find a place for them to meet. Jesus said, "You will find a man walking down the street carrying a pitcher of water. Follow him to the house where he will go. When you get to the house, the owner will show you a room, all ready for the meal."

Peter and John did as Jesus said and found the room all ready. Then Jesus and the other disciples came and they all sat down together.

Jesus said to them, "I have looked forward to this time with you." He knew His time to die was coming soon. He told His disciples that this would be the last time He would eat with them.

Then Jesus took a glass of wine and thanked God for it. Then He shared it with all of His disciples. Next He took a loaf of bread and thanked God for it. Then He passed it around for them all to eat from. Jesus told them to eat a meal like this often to help them remember Him.

Jesus knew He would die on the cross soon. This last time He ate with the disciples was to help them remember Him. We call this last meal Jesus ate The Lord's Supper.

(Luke 22:7-19)

Questions:
1) What happened at the Passover Meal Jesus ate with His disciples?
2) What did Jesus know was going to happen soon?
3) What did Jesus tell the disciples to do as they ate the meal?

Jesus Prays in the Garden

When Jesus and His disciples left the room where they ate the Passover meal, Jesus took them to a lovely old garden. It was in a grove of olive trees.

Jesus told the disciples to sit down and wait while He went on ahead to pray. He took Peter, James, and John with Him.

Jesus was very, very sad. He knew the time for Him to die was getting very close. He knew He was going to die. He knew this because He is God's Son. Jesus knows everything.

Jesus said to Peter and James and John, "Stay awake with me while I'm praying." Then He went on ahead a little into the garden. He fell to His knees and prayed, "Father, if it can be, don't let this awful death happen to me. But I want what you want for me." Jesus knew He had to die. He would die for the sins of the world. He knew there was no other way we could have our sins taken away. So He was willing to die for us because He loved us.

After Jesus prayed, He went back over to where Peter, James, and John were waiting. And do you know what? He found them asleep! He wakened Peter and said, "Peter, couldn't you even stay awake with me for one hour?" This must have made Jesus even more sad.

Jesus wants us all to pray often. He wants us to ask for God's help in the things we do. He wants us to pray often to God just as He did.

(Matthew 26:36-41)

Questions:
1) Who did Jesus take to pray with Him?
2) What did He tell them to do while He was praying?
3) Did the disciples stay awake?
4) How did this make Jesus feel?

Peter Says He Doesn't Know Jesus

The soldiers had come to take Jesus away. They came into the garden where He had been praying with His disciples. They came carrying lighted torches, for it was nighttime.

The soldiers took Jesus and tied His hands and led Him to the house of the high priest. They were going to ask Him some questions there. Peter followed a little behind the crowd that led Jesus away.

The soldiers had lit a little fire in the courtyard of the house, for the night was cool. Peter stood there by the fire. A young girl saw him and said, "This man was with Jesus!" Peter said, "Woman, I don't even know the man!"

After a while someone else said, "You must be one of them." Again Peter said he was not.

About an hour later, someone looked at Peter and said, "I know this fellow is one of Jesus' disciples, for both are from Galilee." Peter said, "Man, I don't know what you're talking about!" And just as he said those words somewhere nearby a rooster crowed.

At that moment Jesus turned and looked at Peter. Peter remembered what Jesus had said to him at their last meal together. "Before the rooster crows tomorrow morning, you will say three times that you don't know me."

Peter turned and walked out of the courtyard, crying bitterly. He had claimed that he didn't know his friend Jesus, the Son of God!

(Luke 22:47-62)

Questions:
1) Where did the soldiers take Jesus?
2) What did Peter say three times?
3) How do you think Jesus felt?

Jesus Before the Angry Crowd

Jesus was taken to Pilate, the most important ruler in that part of the land. He was the one who would have to say Jesus had to die. The people started telling what they thought Jesus had been doing wrong. "He has been telling the people not to pay their taxes! He has been claiming He is our king! He has been upsetting crowds of people," they all yelled.

"Are you their king?" Pilate asked Jesus. "Yes, it is as you say," said Jesus.

Then Pilate called the leaders together and told them he could find nothing Jesus had done that was wrong. But the crowd yelled, "Kill him, Kill him!" Pilate argued with them, for he wanted to let Jesus go free. But they kept shouting, "Kill him!"

Once more Pilate told the people that Jesus hadn't done anything wrong, but they wouldn't listen to him. So he finally said Jesus must die on the cross.

Pilate had Jesus whipped on the back with a heavy whip. The soldiers made a crown of thorns and cruelly pushed it down on His head. They put a long purple robe on Him and made fun of Him. They hit Him with their fists.

Through all this, Jesus didn't say a word. The people were very cruel to Him. But Jesus knew He had to die. That was why He came to this world.

(John 18:28-19:16)

Questions:
1) Who was Pilate?
2) What did the angry crowd want Pilate to do to Jesus?
3) Did Pilate want to have Jesus killed?

Jesus Dies on the Cross

Jesus was given over to the crowd. They had made a heavy wooden cross and made Him carry it through the streets of the city. The cross was so heavy the soldiers made another man help Jesus carry it.

When they got outside the city to a high hill, they crucified Jesus. This means they nailed Him to the cross so He would die. There were two bad men crucified also—one on either side of Jesus.

When Jesus was hanging there on the cross, He said to God, "Father, please forgive these people who are doing this to me—for they don't know what they're doing!"

The soldiers made fun of Jesus. "If you are the king, save yourself and come down from the cross." One of the men being crucified with Jesus said, "Jesus, remember me when you get to heaven." Jesus said to him, "Today you will be with me in heaven."

At noon, the sky went dark. The darkness lasted for three long hours. Then Jesus shouted, "Father, I give my spirit to you." And then He died.

Many people stood around crying. They were very sad because Jesus was dead.

A good man asked Pilate if he could have the body of Jesus. He took it down off the cross and got it ready for burial. Then he placed Jesus' body in a new tomb carved out of a big rock on the side of a hill.

Jesus died because He loved us. He died for the sins of the whole world.

(Luke 23:26-56)

Questions:
1) What did Jesus ask God to do for the people who were crucifying Him?
2) What did Jesus say to the man being crucified with Him?
3) Where did they put Jesus' body?
4) Why did Jesus die on the cross?

Jesus Is Alive

Early Sunday morning, while it was still dark, Mary went to the tomb where Jesus had been buried. To her great surprise, the heavy stone that covered the opening to the tomb had been rolled away! Mary could not understand how this could have happened.

She ran into town and found Peter and John and said, "They have taken the Lord's body out of the tomb. I don't know where they have taken Him!"

Peter and John ran to the tomb. They found the graveclothes, but Jesus' body was gone!

Peter and John went on home and soon Mary came back to the tomb. She stood just outside, and she was crying. As she was there, she looked into the empty tomb. To her surprise, she saw two angels in white robes sitting at the head and the foot of the place where Jesus' body had been.

"Why are you crying?" they asked. "Because they have taken my Lord. And I don't know where!" Mary told them.

Mary looked over her shoulder and saw someone standing behind her. It was Jesus, but she didn't know it! "Why are you crying? Who are you looking for?" He asked. Mary thought He was the gardener.

"Mary!" Jesus said. Mary turned and looked at Jesus. "Master!" she said. "Go and tell my disciples that I'm going to my Father," said Jesus.

Mary ran quickly and told the disciples that Jesus was alive! She had seen Him and talked to Him!

(John 20:1-18)

Questions:
1) Who was the woman who came to the tomb?
2) Did Mary have any idea what happened to Jesus' body?
3) When Jesus spoke to Mary, who did she think He was?
4) What did Jesus tell Mary to do?

God Sends His Holy Spirit

Before Jesus went back to heaven He told His disciples, "When the Holy Spirit has come upon you, you will receive power to tell others about me, to the people where you live, and nearby, and then all over the world."

It had been seven weeks now since Jesus died and rose again. All of the believers in Jesus were meeting together in one place. Suddenly there was a sound like a great wind-storm! The sound filled the room! Then, what looked like little flames of fire settled down on the heads of everybody in the room!

Everyone there was filled with God's Holy Spirit! They began speaking words they didn't know. People outside heard the strange noises and came inside to see. Some thought the believers were drunk! But Peter said to them, "We're not drunk. What you see here the prophets long ago said would happen. God's Spirit has come upon us."

Then Peter preached a long sermon, telling about Jesus. And many, many people believed in Jesus that day and were baptized.

The believers met together often. They always shared what they had with each other. They worshiped together in the temple and met in each other's homes to remember Jesus. They shared their meals with each other. They were very thankful and praised God! And every day more people believed in Jesus!

(Acts 1:8-3:44)

Questions:
1) What did Jesus promise would happen to His followers when the Holy Spirit came upon them?
2) What happened when the Holy Spirit came upon the people in the room?
3) What did Peter begin to do?

An Angel Sets Peter Free

Wicked King Herod had Peter arrested for preaching about Jesus. He was put in prison and had sixteen soldiers guarding him!

The Christians, or people who believed in Jesus the Christ, prayed every day for Peter. They prayed that God would keep him safe while he was in prison.

There in the prison, Peter was sleeping one night. He was double chained between two soldiers, and other soldiers were guarding the gate to the prison. Suddenly, there was a light in Peter's room. An angel was standing there beside him! The angel woke him up and said, "Get up, Peter!" Peter's chains fell off! The angel said, "Get dressed and follow me!" Peter obeyed the angel.

Peter thought he was having a dream! He and the angel walked past all the guards and all the locked doors opened for them. The guards didn't even know they were there! Then they were out of the prison, on the street. They walked along for a while, and the angel disappeared! Then Peter knew he wasn't having a dream. It was real! God had sent an angel to get him out of prison!

Peter went to the home of some Christian friends. They were having a prayer meeting and were praying for him. Peter knocked quietly at the front door of the house and a little girl named Rhoda answered. She was so surprised to see Peter! She ran and told everyone! At first they didn't believe her when she said Peter was there. Then they saw it really was him! They all praised and thanked God for Peter's safe release from prison.

(Acts 12:1-17)

Questions:
1) Why did King Herod have Peter put in prison?
2) How did Peter get out of prison?
3) Why do you think the Christians didn't believe it was really Peter at the door?
4) Why do you think God brought Peter out of prison?

Paul Becomes a Helper for Jesus

Paul was a very important man. But he did not like people who loved Jesus. In fact, he tried to hurt them and have them put in jail. He thought he was doing the right thing. He thought he was pleasing God. Paul did not know Jesus was God's Son.

One day Paul was going down the road to another town. Suddenly a bright light from heaven flashed all around him. Paul was very, very scared. He fell down to the ground. Then he heard a voice say, "Paul, why do you keep on hurting Me?" Paul didn't know who was talking to him.

Then Paul said, "Who are you?" The Voice said, "I am Jesus that you keep on hurting."

From that moment on, Paul believed Jesus was God's Son. He loved Jesus very much. He wanted to be Jesus' helper. He stopped hurting people who loved Jesus. He tried to help them instead. Jesus told Paul what He wanted him to do for Him. Paul became one of Jesus' best friends and helpers.

(Acts 9:1-19)

Questions:
1) Who talked to Paul on the road one day?
2) Did Paul become one of Jesus' helpers?
3) How can you be a helper for Jesus?

Paul and Silas in Prison

O nce Paul and Silas had been teaching people about Jesus. A few people who did not love God said they were breaking the law. So Paul and Silas were arrested. The judge ordered them to be beaten with wooden whips. Then they were thrown into prison.

The man who guarded the jail was told if he let Paul and Silas escape he would be killed! He was so worried that he had Paul and Silas put in the inside jail. Then he locked their feet in wooden blocks so they could not walk!

But Paul and Silas were not worried or afraid. They knew God was with them. At midnight they could be heard singing and praying to God! Suddenly, a great earthquake shook the prison! All the locked doors flew open! The chains on every prisoner fell off!

The jailer was very scared when he saw the doors open. He thought every prisoner had escaped. He knew he would be killed if Paul and Silas escaped. So he drew out his sword to kill himself. Suddenly Paul yelled to him, "Don't kill yourself! We're all here!"

The jailer was very, very scared. He ran to Paul and Silas and said, "Sirs, what must I do to be saved?"

Paul and Silas answered, "Believe in the Lord Jesus Christ, and you will be saved, and everyone in your house."

(Acts 16:16-31)

Questions:
1) Why were Paul and Silas arrested?
2) What would happen to the jailer if he let Paul and Silas escape?
3) What did Paul and Silas say to the jailer when he asked how he could be saved?
4) Have you believed in Jesus?